PANORAMIC DARTMOOR

ADRIAN OAKES

HALSGROVE

First published in Great Britain in 2010

British Library Cataloguing-in-Publication Data
A CIP record for this title is available from the British Library

ISBN 978 0 85704 039 8

HALSGROVE
Halsgrove House,
Ryelands Industrial Estate,
Bagley Road, Wellington, Somerset TA21 9PZ
Tel: 01823 653777   Fax: 01823 216796
email: sales@halsgrove.com

Part of the Halsgrove group of companies.
Information on all Halsgrove titles is available at: www.halsgrove.com

Printed and bound in China by Toppan Leefung Printing Ltd

Right: The distinctive rock outcrop of Bowerman's Nose. In legend the rock is said to be the hunter Bowerman turned to stone by witches when his hounds disturbed them, and the numerous stones littered around the base are the hounds.

INTRODUCTION

FOR AS LONG AS I have been interested in landscape photography, I have always enjoyed the 'wider view'. Although landscape views are wonderful and exciting to capture, the wide panoramic image can display so much more of the vista. A bit less sky but much more to see.

When you stand and admire a landscape you see it in a panoramic format, thus an image seen this way suits your field of view.

I have been photographing Devon and Dartmoor panoramas for many years and although they are more of a technical challenge, it is immensely rewarding when the end result is a highly detailed image that looks better the larger it is seen.

My inspiration for this book has come from the desire to express my appreciation of the Dartmoor landscapes in this elongated format. Striving to capture that special image can be very rewarding and when it is achieved it makes up for the many mornings waiting patiently for the light, only for a bank of cloud to appear and spoil the show. I find the best times are when the sun is low in the sky especially in autumn and early winter.

From the open high moorland and ancient moss-coated woodlands to snow covered tors, I have hiked many miles in all weathers and seasons to capture this collection of images. One of my favourite aspects of the moor are the views from the tops of the tors from many of which you have an uninterrupted view for miles in all directions. I have included some of these views in this collection and most of the panoramas are of at least 180 degree field of view.

Returning home from the moor, I feel tired but exhilarated from the exercise, having enjoyed the views and the general mood and atmosphere. Long walks to find that panoramic view with something special in the foreground while carrying a heavy tripod and a rucksack with two cameras, five lenses, filters and 'life support items' such as hot drinks and extra layers of clothing takes a toll, but it is worth every step.

The moor will always be to me a place to spend quality time as I am sure many others will agree, and I will continue to visit and photograph Dartmoor for many years.

Adrian Oakes 2010
www.adrianoakes.com

From experience in the field I have found Dartmoor regularly offers some of the most impressive displays of bluebells on open ground away from the cover offered in the woods. This favourite area of mine is at Emsworthy just beyond Saddle Tor. The area is an old farm settlement with walled pastures which fill with a wonderful carpet of blue in late May.

A favourite waterfall that I visit often sits in Tavy Cleave near the pool known as 'Devils Kitchen' A reasonable walk from Lanehead car park, along the leat and down into the cleave and eventually you will come across the fall. This image was taken after three day's of rainfall resulting in a heavy flow down the cleave. A long exposure using filters creates the effect in the water flow.

Overleaf: One of my most popular images. This picture is taken from one of the highest points on Great Staple Tor just before sunset in late autumn. Many other tors can been seen in the distance including Vixen Tor, Feather Tor, King Tor, Sharpitor, Sheepstor and Hucken Tor.

A short climb from the road led me past this attractive vantage point with the disused Merrivale granite quarry in the distance. This quarry was closed in the mid 1990s and produced granite for many buildings in Devon and notably the Old London Bridge now sited in Arizona.

A long walk around the Fernworthy forest area led me towards the Grey Wethers stone circles. As the weather started to close in over the forest in the distance I returned through this gateway which caught my eye as the ancient stone wall stretched into the distant mist.

Dramatic skies over the northern moor from a high vantage point near Willingstone Rock just after sunrise. The Teign valley including Fingle Bridge sits below. Drewsteignton can be seen with its church just left of centre. I particularly enjoyed the rich and warm autumn colours of the foliage.

Above: Howell Tor in midwinter with Haytor sitting in the distance.

Opposite, above: This is how wonderful Dartmoor can look with a fresh blanket of snow under blue skies and a warm winter sun. The photograph wcs taken at Saddle Tor before any footprints appeared apart from those of a few sheep. Haytor can be see in the far distance.

Opposite, below: A contrasting view from Saddle Tor in late summer. A lovely clear day and good light allows all the colours of the rocks to show.

A hike around the Bellever area towards the tor led me through the forest. This image wasn't planned but the composition was pleasing with the attractive sky, long shadows and the track twisting away into the trees. Pleasing compositions are often chanced upon. I always keep an open mind when walking.

Overleaf: This is one of my planned shots from a walk around Bellever forest. The low sun illuminates the forest floor and the rich greens of the thick moss that coats virtually every surface.

One of my favourite views from Great Staple Tor which I try to visit regularly. A different image can taken on virtually every visit. A very swift hike to the top allowed a few minutes of rich winter colour to silhouette the tor just after sunset.

Bellever Tor surrounded in heather and gorse in full bloom in late summer.

I have often tried to capture Bennett's Cross with snow drifts and finally managed in the winter of 2010. Birch Tor is hidden in the mist on the horizon.

Above: Sheep graze in the bluebells with early summer blossom on the trees.

Opposite, above: Old winch gear lies in Haytor quarry in midwinter. The quarry was fully operational from around 1819 and produced granite for many decades before closing. It was briefly reopened in 1919 for stone to build the Exeter War Memorial.

Opposite, below: Becky Falls in midwinter. The rocks were covered in foot-long icicles.

A blustery spring day at Hound Tor. Nearby sits another famous landmark, Bowerman's Nose.

Grey Wethers stone circles beyond Fernworthy on a misty day. The site was excavated in 1898 and the area within the circles was found to contain charcoal. The circles are in very good condition as a result of restoration in 1909.

A climb up to Sharpitor rewarded me with this beautiful vista and dramatic sky. Peek Hill and the path leading up to it lie in the distance.

Greator rocks lie just south-east of Hound Tor. A very steep climb to the top, not recommended with tripod and camera gear, allowed me to capture the peak of the rocks. It reminded me of the top of a volcano. Hound Tor is in the distance.

Lone tree near Saddle Tor in midsummer.

A winter view from Bench Tor above the Dart Valley. Venford reservoir sits amongst the trees to the left. Sharp Tor can just be seen on the horizon to the far right.

Overleaf: A steep climb up the side of the hill on to Yennadon Down gave me a clear view across Burrator with the prominent bulk of Sheepstor beyond.

Vixen Tor shrouded in low lying mist, with King Tor in the distance.

Bonehill rocks above the East Webburn river valley. I had camped here a few times but had never photographed it. It is a quite striking set of rocks set high above the road and offering views across Widecombe-in-the-Moor. Bell Tor and Chinkwell Tor sit just beyond to the right.

Above: Just after the heaviest snow of the winter the roads were clear enough to drive across the moor. A walk up to the top of a hill in two feet of snow gave forth this great view of Sharp Tor just after sunset with lovely muted colours.

Opposite, above: View in early winter over the Dart Valley from Combestone Tor. A lone weathered tree adds to the composition.

Opposite, below: Autumn colours on the River Teign.

The Giant's Chair sits on private land above the East Webburn river valley looking south towards Widecombe-in-the-Moor. At thirty-feet in height, the chair shows true craftsmanship and adds something original and special to the moor. Haytor can been seen on the horizon to the left. I took this picture from the footpath leading from Jay's Grave.

The Bronze Age settlement at Grimspound possesses a truly unique atmosphere. The circular ring of stones which would originally have been a wall enclose an area of about four acres and would have housed settlers and livestock. Remains of huts and animal enclosures can been seen within the circle. This photograph shows the main entrance into the settlement with Hookney Tor above. This dramatic gateway lends itself to a panoramic composition.

Overleaf: Spooky ancient woodland and stunted oaks in early winter when the sun struggles to pierce the dense canopy. An inch-thick carpet of moss coats everything. I am sure if I stood still too long it would start growing on my boots.

A bright day from the trig point on Bellever Tor looking over the forest. I love days like this with good skies, rich colour and clear visibility. Princetown sits on the horizon just above the trig point.

A trek on to the moor in the harsh winter of early 2010 rewarded me with many great views including this one looking across the valley towards Chagford Common. The mist creeps over the distant hills towards me.

Late afternoon light at a small clapper bridge at Wallabrook. Dartmoor has many clapper bridges, the best known being Postbridge. Scorhill circle is in the far left distance.

This wouldn't normally be a panoramic composition I would take but the lone rowan tree caught my eye. Sitting against the backdrop of the forest in a flash of red amongst the rich colours of the heather and gorse, I found this really worked for me as a Dartmoor view.

A gateway I have passed and photographed many times in ice, snow and rain. It makes for an easy composition with Rippon Tor sitting in the background. I particularly like this one for the contrast in the stone wall in the late afternoon light and the threatening sky. Late in the day is the best time to photograph the moorland rocks as the low light picks out the surface and colours of the granite

A blanket of low-lying mist in the valley bottom catches the morning sun near Moretonhampstead. I always try to get out with the camera on mornings like this and thus have many shots of mist on Dartmoor and in Devon. This one has a peaceful and ethereal quality.

Postbridge clapper bridge. I took this from a low perspective to capture the newer road bridge under the span of the older one. Such clapper bridges can be found all over the moor, some in isolated locations.

Pew Tor with a winding path leading away to the east.

Autumn colours along the River Teign valley. I stood on a very precarious small jetty in the middle of the river for this photo. There was just enough room for me and an enormous tripod.

Buckland church with its unusual clock faces that have no numbers. When you are there next take a look and see. A small group of old thatched cottages sit nearby.

The impressive village sign stands at the entrance to Widecombe-in-the-Moor in midwinter.

Sitting among conifer plantations Blackingstone Rock, with its moon-like surface, provides an interesting spot for a panorama. Iron steps lead to the summit. It is a great location especially early in the day. Three other photographers with their tripods waited patiently behind me as I quickly composed this panorama.

Haytor panorama taken a few years ago. The day on the moor had been a disappointment with cloud and poor light but as I headed off the moor the light started to change so I turned round and went back on a fine autumn evening.

Previous page: Dartmoor has hundreds of prehistoric remains, including hut circles such as this one. These are the remains of dwellings that have long since lost their roofs. This one sits high up on Shapley Common.

Above: A snow-covered footbridge deep in the valley below Becky Falls.

Opposite, above: I have visited Buckland and the bridge there many times, but on this particular day there was a torrent running beneath which lent itself well to long exposures. The autumn leaves and moss add wonderful colour-tones and texture.

Opposite, below: Postbridge in the snow and devoid of visitors. I had it all to myself for ages...

Hexworthy Bridge and the river Dart.

I have a fascination with valleys and mist. This one was well worth the exhausting climb to the top of the hill for the view point. You don't need to be near the mist to get shots like this. The key is to be high up with a good zoom lens and a tripod.

A thick blanket of mist in the Teign Valley, taken from the fringes of Dartmoor.

Thatched houses nestling in a Dartmoor valley at Buckland in autumn.

Dense greenery surrounds a gorge on the northern moor. Dartmoor has many hidden gorges flanked with ferns and trees.

Rich autumn colours near the footbridge along from Fingle bridge in the Teign Valley.

A long day on the moor was nearly at an end and the sky wasn't looking good for the sunset. I was high on the moor so a brisk climb to the top rewarded me with a superb quality of light just as the sun set over Tavistock.

A trip up on to the Moor last thing in midwinter rewarded me with an amazing soft light just after sunset that gave the landscape a light magenta hue.

North Bovey, with its thatched cottages and village green, is one of the most attractive small villages on Dartmoor. Here the church of St John is set against a threatening and dramatic sky.

One of Dartmoor's most common but interesting features are its thousands of miles of ancient drystone walls. I especially like the way they snake across the countryside into the distance. I walked along this one returning from Buckland Beacon one sunny afternoon. Rippon Tor can be seen on the horizon centre left.

Overleaf: Some of the most dramatic open views can be found on the northern side of the moor, such as here looking from Higher Tor over Belstone Common.

Hookney Tor near Grimspound looking towards Widecombe in the Moor.

Ancient stunted oaks at Wistman's Wood. Legend tells of how the wood is inhabited by black hounds and it is said to be the most haunted place on the moor. I have visited early, just before sunrise, and its not a very comfortable feeling to be alone in the wood at that hour.

As I left Dartmeet I happened to glance back to see this tree. A while spent composing the shot to capture the amazing sky resulted in this image. Dartmeet sits in the valley shrouded in dense mist.

A collection of Rowan trees in full colour stand out against the green firs. Many Tors can be seen on the horizon above the tree line including Higher White Tor and Beardown Tor.

Overleaf: View from Meldon Hill over Chagford. A rain cloud opens on the horizon and was heading my way so I hastily headed back to the car.

A Trig point looking towards Shapley Common. Fernworthy forest can be seen on the horizon to the far right.

A difficult walk in snow up to the top of my wellies eventually gave me a good spot to capture the thick snow coating on the gorse below Haytor.

Dartmoor possesses many wonderful rivers and falls. The River Dart is especially beautiful in early summer.

View across Burrator from Leather Tor. A dramatic sky was gradually thickening with rain already falling in the distance.

Overleaf: I was pondering where to go next when I looked out across the fringes of the moor to see this amazing cloud formation from the top of Whitchurch Common towards Tavistock. The sun was just about to break under the cloud when I took the picture.

I have often travelled to Merrivale hoping to catch the stone rows in the snow. I was lucky on this day as the light was also wonderful.

Tottiford Reservoir reflections on a still late summer day. Dartmoor has a number of such reservoirs often set amid attractive scenery surrounded by woodland.

A frozen snow-filled Dartmoor valley. A precarious climb was well worth it to reach the river for a series of amazing shots of huge icicles, rocks and snow.

A rushing Dartmoor river in deep snow and ice..

Blue sunset over the moor with melting snow against drystone walls.

Opposite, above: An ancient moss-covered stone wall with what looks like a half-buried mill stone.

Opposite, below: Bellever Bridge sits next to an ancient clapper bridge near Postbridge. The clapper is partially collapsed.

Combestone Tor – one of the most accessible on the moor, and giving spectacular views over the Dart Valley.

Photos often come when unexpected. Whilst heading across the moor I was greeted with this view of Great Staple Tor and Great Mis Tor poking out of the mist on the horizon.

The tiny church of St Michael de Rupe sits on top of the rocky outcrop of Brentor, 1130 feet above sea level. Founded in the thirteenth century, regular services are still held here. I have visited this superb photographic location many times and on this day I was lucky with the light.

Overleaf: A fantastic view across the moor from Widgery Cross. I had to clamber around on the various rocks for quite a while to capture the vista with the cross in view.

In Lydford Parish looking towards Bray Tor, Arms Tor, Tavy Cleave Tors and Ger Tor.

The North Teign rushes over rocks in early Winter.

Lady Exmouth Fall at Canonteign. Englands tallest waterfall.

One of my favourite Winter panoramas of Dartmoor: the dramatic sky and the silhouetted trees enveloped in drifting snow and mist, with Dartmoor ponies grazing in the field.

On a misty morning its sometimes possible to get above it by climbing a tor high on the open moor. This particular morning the whole area was covered in a thick blanket of fog. From the top of the tor I had a clear view of the horizon and was rewarded with the most wonderful light as the sun rose and lit up the surface of the mist. The light-show lasted no more than five minutes. Bovey Tracey is hidden under the mist.